Poland travel guide 2024

Poland: Embrace the Unseen - Crafting Itineraries, Exploring Must-Sees, and Chasing Adventure

Alex J. Cook

Copyright

All right reserved, no part of this publication may be reproduced, distributed or transmitted in any form or by any means. Including photocopying, recording or other electronic or mechanical methods without the prior written permission of the publisher, except in the case of brief questions embodied in critical reviews and certain other noncommercial uses permitted by copyright law. Copyright © Alex J Cook, 2024

About the author

Alex J Cook, a seasoned globetrotter and wordsmith, is your compass to the world's wonders. With a passion for exploration and a knack for uncovering hidden gems, Cook's travel guides seamlessly blend practical advice with vivid storytelling. Whether navigating bustling markets in Marrakech or trekking serene trails in Patagonia, Cook's insightful narratives and curated tips promise to turn any journey into an unforgettable adventure. Embark on a discovery-filled odyssey with Alex J Cook as your trusted guide to the world's diverse landscapes and cultures.

Table Of Contents

Introduction.. 11

Chapter 1: Poland — History and Culture. 18

- **Poland Occasions and Celebrations... 23**

Chapter 2: 10 Things You Need to Pack for Your Trip to Poland............................29

- **Visa requirements**............................ 38
- **20 Tips for Low-Budget Travel Around Poland**................................. 49

Chapter 3: Best Time to Visit Poland...... 67

Chapter 4: 1 Week in Poland: An itinerary for first-time visitors................................. 85

Chapter 5: 20+ Best Things To Do In Poland.. 111

Chapter 6: 14 Best Places to Visit in Poland..139

Chapter 7: 10 Best Polish Foods Everyone Should Try...161

Chapter 8:12 Restaurants In Poland That Will Make You Fall In Love With Polish Cuisine..169

Chapter 9: 7 non-touristy cities to discover in southern Poland.................. 181
Chapter 10: Safety and security.............191
- **Top travel and tourism Websites for 2024.................................. 204**

Conclusion...208

Welcome to Poland 2024

Welcome to "Poland: Embrace the Concealed," your identification to a phenomenal excursion through the core of this charming country. In the pages that follow, we welcome you to investigate Poland in a manner that goes past the common, finding a rich embroidery woven with history, culture, and secret marvels.

As you set out on this experience, our aide turns into your believed friend, offering custom schedules that take care of each and every explorer's taste. From the magnificent roads of Warsaw to the middle-age appeal of Krakow and the sea charm of Gdansk, every section unfurls a consistent mix of must-see milestones and off in an unexpected direction treasure.

Be that as it may, this guide is something other than a schedule; it's a challenge to wander past the self-evident. We allure you to investigate stowed-away experiences in the dim Tatra Mountains and the peaceful pools of Masuria, uncovering the untold accounts of Poland's regular wonder.

Submerge yourself in a Clean culture, relishing the kinds of customary cooking, participating in neighborhood customs, and encountering the certifiable warmth of individuals. Our aide fills in as a door to the essence of Poland, rejuvenating the practices, celebrations, and customs that characterize this dazzling objective.

As you flip through these pages, let the accounts unfurl - stories that rise above time, winding around together the past, present, and fate of Poland. Whether you're a set of experiences fan, a daring soul, or a culture devotee, "Poland: Embrace the Concealed" guarantees an excursion that reverberates with your inclinations and makes a permanent imprint on your movement recollections.

In this way, diagram your own course, enable your investigation, and reclassify your view of Poland. This guide is an open greeting to jump into the core of Poland's excellence, variety, and appeal. Is it true that you are prepared to embrace the inconspicuous? Your unmatched Clean experience is standing by. Welcome to an excursion that rises above assumptions.

Introduction

Poland Overview

Poland is home to seemingly the world's most charming history. Multiple times the nation arrived in the possession of another European power, and this was exclusively from the eighteenth century onwards. Regardless of this, there is as yet a predominant public character and remarkable culture.

Poland sits in Central Europe, lined toward the North by the Baltic Ocean. It is quite possibly one of the most different countries in Europe with regards to spots to see and exercises to appreciate. Warsaw is the political, business, and monetary capital and home to a brilliant Old Town that was remarkably reconstructed out of the rubble following The Second Great War. Krakow is the social focus of Poland and the previous capital. Its focal region is a UNESCO World Legacy site, and worth looking at for a couple of days. For additional middle-age attractions, go on an outing to the scaffolds of Wroclaw and the Renaissance-roused engineering of Lublin. With the new rapid rail connecting various urban areas across Poland, seeing every one of these across-the-board trips is unquestionably reasonable.

Poland's part in The Second Great War was more horrendous and wild than some other country on The planet, and visiting the notorious Auschwitz camps will leave an enduring memory. For a more perky encounter, Bialowieza Public Park, Bory Tucholskie Public Park, and the fountain-filled Karkanoski Public Park are among the main normal attractions in the country.

Costs for accommodations have gone up essentially lately, and that implies that Poland is as of now not the deal spot it used to be. Significant urban areas like Krakow and Warsaw have bigger inn networks and less expensive choices. Get your work done however on the grounds that a portion of the inns are famous issue spots, with reports of messy offices and senseless curfews. Brew is the beverage of decision among local people, albeit Russian vodkas are common at most clubs and bars. Food in Poland is very special, and there are various customary dishes that can be tested all through the urban communities.

Poland encounters a calm environment. Because of its situation between the Baltic Ocean and the European Alps, the nation has a mainland climate in the south and maritime impacts in the north. Precipitation for the most part happens all year, yet there is considerably more precipitation in the colder time of year (December through February) than in late spring (June through August). Winter is cold, with temperatures averaging 21°F. Summer is gentle to warm, with midpoints somewhere in the range of 70°F and 80°F.

Warsaw Chopin Worldwide Air terminal is the nation's significant door. Notwithstanding, there are a few other occupied air terminals that invite more than 1,000,000 travelers every year, including Krakow and Katowice. Most homegrown flights are presented through Parcel Poland Carriers, which traverses the country with short-pull flights. Going into Poland via train is likewise conceivable from significant urban communities in Germany, the Netherlands, Russia, Austria, and the Czech

Republic. Nonetheless, the least expensive method for arriving in Poland is by transport.

Despite the fact that Poland's framework has worked over recent years, the nation actually comes up short on an effective thruway/motorway framework. With the absence of simple to-explore streets, Poland isn't the least demanding spot to get around via vehicle. Gridlocks are deteriorating each year, which makes the strategies of driving ominous.

Highlights
- Investigate the old salt mines of Wieliczka
- Find the abhorrences of life for detainees of Auschwitz
- Unwind upon the sea shores of the Baltic coast
- Tour the amazing fountains of Karkonoski Public Park

- Ski Zakopane's runs during the virus cold weather months
- Cycle through the Old Town locale of Poland's middle age wonders

Chapter 1: Poland — History and Culture

Poland has one of the world's most huge public chronicles. When a flourishing European province, the nation radically tumbled from its platform, at last vanishing out and out toward the eighteenth century's end. By the by, public pride and a special personality is savagely present.

History
Poland truly grew up during the fourteenth and sixteenth 100 years. At that point, the Clean Lithuanian Republic was the biggest and most prosperous country on the European mainland. The capital, which was situated in Krakow for over 500 years, moved to Warsaw toward the finish of the next 100 years. Be that as it may, many

conflicts with unfamiliar powers truly crushed the economy, creating critical political issues.

In the last part of the 1800s, Poland was divided by all the more remarkable neighbors: Austria, Prussia, and Russia. The occupation prompted an expansion in industrialization and efficiency for the economy, however subsequently, Poland failed to exist as a country for over 120 years starting in 1795. Stifling the Clean public character and culture brought about savage uprisings and in the end, they recovered autonomy following Germany's acquiescence in 1918. The ensuing area divisions prompted a proceeded crack between Germany, Austria, and even Czechoslovakia (Slovakia/Czech Republic).

Poland was attacked by Germany and Russia again in September 1939, at first starting

WWII. Despite the fact that the Clean Republic was re-lighted just a short time previously, it again stopped existing during and after the conflict. Shocking atrocities were knowledgeable about Poland somewhere in the range of 1939 and 1945, with the nation losing 20% of its populace. Travelers can in any case visit the most scandalous death camps including the famous Auschwitz (Więźniów Oświęcimia 20, Oświęcim, Poland).

Following WWII, Poland strongly turned into a Soviet-Socialist state and was known as the Individuals' Republic of Poland. Regardless of the times of financial development, the 1950s through to the 1980s saw frightful downturns, remembering those for 1956 and 1976. In the 1980s, hostile to Socialist workers organizations, especially Fortitude started to go against the public authority. Obviously, the Soviets answered with military contribution and cinched down on political exercises against the state. By and by, the worker's organization's activities debilitated the public authority's power, in the long run prompting free-vote races by 1989.

Current Poland is a monetary example of overcoming adversity, flaunting major areas of strength for a public personality notwithstanding its tempestuous past. In 1999, Poland turned out to be essential for NATO, and by 2004, was an individual from the European Association. For a more nitty gritty gander at the country's new history, visit Poland's Public Historical Center (Aleje Jerozolimskie 3, Warsaw, Poland).

Culture
Poland has encountered many dim parts now is the right time. For a really long period, they were constrained by encompassing neighbors including Germany and Russia. In

any case, a significant part of the nearby culture actually prospered under the rule of Prussian and Russian pioneers. A long and lenient history saw Poland become a stronghold of multiculturalism during the seventeenth and eighteenth hundreds of years. Before WWII, Poland was a blend of Catholicism and a few other strict groups. In any case, this changed emphatically following the conflict, with most local people following the Roman Catholic confidence. This religion turned out to be considerably more pervasive after the appointment of Pope John Paul II as the top of the Congregation.

Poland Occasions and Celebrations

The greater part of Poland's famous celebrations connect with the nation's adoration for music. Poland occasions and occasions are generally current happenings, which started after the country's autonomy from Soviet rule in 1989. Jazz is a feature at the All Spirits Jazz Celebration in November and quite possibly the main day on the schedule is Freedom Day, which praises their latest freedom from Socialism.

Cracovia Long distance race
During the springtime month of April, Krakow has the mainland Cracovia long-distance race. There is the full long-distance race for no-nonsense sprinters, and more limited distances for others to partake in.

Constitution Day
In 1791, Poland's subsequent constitution was drawn up and carried out. Commended on May 3, the day incorporates different intriguing merriments and is ordinarily gotten together with Work Day on May 1.

Worldwide Road Workmanship Celebration

July's Worldwide Road Workmanship Celebration is a sublime method for encountering nearby cultures in Warsaw. It is quite possibly the most extraordinary festival in Europe, with the roads of the capital the background of many showcases and exhibitions happening just before your eyes.

Junction Celebration

The Junction Celebration is held in the city of Krakow consistently in July. The occasion is renowned for bringing a scope of music from around the world, including the exceptional preferences of Mongolia, Israel, Eastern Europe, and the Center East.

Jazz at the Old Town

Jazz at the Old Town Celebration is a striking live melodic occasion that brings a large number of craftsmanship darlings from across Poland and Europe. It is hung on Saturday nights in July and August, so guests are ensured a warm climate for the occasion. The celebration is held at Warsaw's Old Town and is allowed to join in.

Warsaw Worldwide Film Celebration
Thousands run to the Warsaw Film Celebration consistently in October, an extraordinary method for expanding the limits and arriving at film darlings and types across the globe. The movies and appearances are presented in various settings, and a lot of gatherings are held at the ends of the week for guests to the occasion.

Freedom Day
Ostensibly the greatest and most significant festival on the Clean schedule, Freedom Day in November is the remembrance of Poland's liberation from Russian occupation. Since the mid-1990s, this radiant celebration has seen

significant urban communities and towns celebrate in their own particular manner. Warsaw is the spot to be however for firecrackers, exhibitions, food, and rides all through the capital.

All Spirits Jazz Celebration

Situated in the city of Krakow every November, the All Spirits Jazz Celebration pulls in huge groups all through its activity. The occasion has developed into one of the nation's biggest and most renowned melodic occasions.

Chapter 2: 10 Things You Need to Pack for Your Trip to Poland

What to Pack for Your Outing to Poland

1. Visa

This is the main thing you want for your excursion to Poland. On the off chance that you fail to remember your identification, you really won't make it into Poland as you will be dismissed at the air terminal entryway in the US.

Residents of the US don't need a movement visa to enter Poland. Something that not every person knows about is that your visa Should BE Legitimate for somewhere around 90 days past your date of entry into the country. It is critical to take note that Americans are simply permitted to go to

Poland (or some other Schengen Country) for 90 days out of 180 days.

2. Cash

While making a trip to Poland it is critical to bring cash as no wherever acknowledges Visas. The nearby money in Poland is called złoty. There are two primary ways of trading US dollars into Clean złoty. In the US, there are money trade workplaces, as well as banks (like Wells Fargo), that will trade American cash into Clean cash. Ensure that you check the ongoing conversion scale as well as the expense that the establishment is charging to guarantee the best rate.

There are additionally numerous money trade workplaces in Poland. Here you should be significantly more fastidious to ensure that you are not getting ripped off. At the point when you travel with us, we vow to find you the best trade office that won't exploit you.

There are likewise many spots in Poland that acknowledge Mastercards. Ensure that you let your Visa organization know that you are voyaging so they don't obstruct your card for dubious worldwide action. It is likewise significant to check in the event that your Visa has a worldwide exchange charge. This expense can be very costly and will charge you a rate or fixed sum each time you utilize your card. There are many Mastercards that offer no worldwide exchange expenses.

3. Cell Phone

All things considered, when you make a trip you intend to carry your cell phone with you. Preceding travel we suggest checking with your telephone organization and setting up a global telephone plan. Contingent upon your organization, these plans can be costly, however it is smart to have something set up, basically for crisis use. Assuming you utilize your telephone without a worldwide arrangement, it tends to be extremely costly.

While it is conceivable in other European nations, it is undeniably challenging in Poland to get a neighborhood SIM card to place on your telephone. Assuming you are hoping to associate your telephone with wifi, most cafés, bistros, lodgings, and even urban communities offer complimentary wireless internet that you can interface with on your telephone.

4. Power Connector

Poland involves similar power connectors as numerous different nations in Europe. This two-dimensional attachment is at times called "C" or "E" and runs on 230V. Noticing the distinction between a power connector and a power converter is significant. With a power connector, you can plug your American gadget straightforwardly into the connector, which connects to the wall (ensure this gadget is upheld by 230V!). A power converter really changes the force of the gadget (120V in the US).

There are a few gadgets that convert power consequently like many sorts of cell phones. Take the iPhone for instance. Here you can simply plug the USB end into a European fitting with a USB space. Be exceptionally cautious while utilizing a power connector and guarantee that your gadget can run on 230V. Most hair dryers, level irons, and so forth won't work. These things can start and, surprisingly, shut off the power.

5. Travel Health care coverage

Travel Health care coverage is essential for your excursion to Poland. Check with your health care coverage in the US to see what their inclusion is globally. On the off chance that fundamental, you might have to buy travel health care coverage from an outsider provider.

FYI the crisis number in Poland is 112.

6. Duplicates of Movement Reports
It is a truly smart thought to bring printed versions of your movement records. This incorporates duplicates of your visa, ID card, boarding passes, inn reservations, and so on. It is likewise a decent tip to snap a picture of the client support number on the rear of your Mastercard. Assuming you lose your card, you can call this number to inform the Mastercard organization. As well as bringing copies of these records, we likewise suggest snapping a picture of them that you keep on your telephone in the event anything occurs.

7. Adaptable Attire
Picking which garments to pack for an outing to Poland may be the most tedious piece of

your pressing! A couple of methods for picking what to bring is to choose clothing things that are flexible and can be worn with various outfits. We likewise suggest bringing layers of dress with the goal that you can be ready for climate and temperature changes.

In Poland, as in different spots in Europe, individuals will quite often be fashionable and assembled. It's smart to bring some pleasant, and furthermore open to, clothing that won't make you stand apart as a voyager.

8. Agreeable Shoes

In Poland, there is such a great amount to see! You would rather not ruin the excursion by having sore feet from awkward shoes. Ensure that your shoes are very much broken in before your outing and that they are agreeable to walk or sub for basically a couple of hours.

9. Day Sack

Having a day sack is smart for movement in Poland. In this pack, you can keep all of your day basics, for example, a wallet, camera, reusable water container, coat, and whatever else you could require over the course of the day. Ensure the sack is little and agreeable to convey while strolling around and investigating the sights!

10. Moving Bag

While picking which bag you ought to bring for your excursion to Poland, we highly suggest one with wheels! Utilizing a bag with wheels will make your movements through air terminals, downtown areas, cabs, and trains a lot simpler. Believe us!

Visa requirements

Substantial visa
Something like 2 clear pages

With the candidate's mark
Not over 10 years of age
Substantial for something like 3 months after the lapse of the mentioned visa
Past identification, if material

Identification estimated photographs
Size 3.5 x 4.5 cm
Plain white foundation
Required inside the beyond a half-year
Front aligned with facial highlights apparent and clear
Finished application structure
Biometric information (Fingerprints)
Visa expense
Reports appropriate to your outing
Travel Agenda or plan
Evidence of return to the nation of home or forward pass to another country
Justification behind the movement to Poland
Flight reservations

Evidence of monetary means (bank articulations over the course of the past 3-month time frame, individual properties, and additionally different resources)

Confirmation of facilities (with booking reference number, area, and contact number of the inn)

Travel clinical protection
Substantial through the whole visa period
Legitimate in all Schengen nations
The least inclusion of 30,000 EUR should be bought
Protection conditions like legitimacy, term, and degree of your inclusion to be plainly expressed on the affirmation letter or protection record

Work letter with the accompanying data:
Name and address of the manager
Nature of work
Beginning date of work

Pay

Motivation behind movement

Length of downtime from work for movement

Filters (duplicates) of:
Individual ID page of visa.
More established Schengen visas (if applicable).
Home license (if applicable).

Candidates under the age of 18 are expected to present the accompanying extra necessities:
Duplicate of birth endorsement
Assuming that the minor candidate is embraced, reception records are required
Assuming that the minor candidate's folks are separated, legal documents are required
Assuming the minor candidate's folks are perished, passing authentications are required

Letter of assent from the two guardians or lawful gatekeepers

Identification duplicates of the two guardians or legitimate watchmen

It might likewise be important to submit valuable records according to your movement visa application.

Poland Schengen Visa Charges

The standard charge for the application for a Poland Schengen visa is 80 EUR. Notwithstanding, there are specific candidates who are absolved from charges, for example, most understudy endlessly visas for kids under the age of 6. Candidates will presumably need to pay a different, non-refundable help installment with their application.

Poland Visa Application Steps

Set up every one of the expected reports.

Select "The travel industry" as the justification behind the movement on the visa application structure.

Conclude the number of sections expected in Poland or the Schengen region.

Finish up the application structure.

The application structure for a Clean Schengen visa can be viewed here. Register for an e-Konsult account, finish up the structure, print, and sign it. The structure should be submitted to the Clean office or visa handling focus.

Plan a visa arrangement, if relevant.

Most applications require an in-person arrangement at the closest Clean Department or visa focus to present the application. Then again, applications might be submitted without earlier arrangements during ordinary working hours. Contact the Clean Department or Visa focus to decide whether there is a need to plan an arrangement.

Another choice is to plan an arrangement online through Poland's E-Konsult website through this connection.

Present your Clean Schengen visa application.

Note: Applications should be submitted something like 15 days before the date of movement yet not sooner than a half year before the date of movement.

By and large, applications should be submitted face to face to the Clean Office or a visa application focus that is associated with Poland. Be that as it may, there might be a couple of contrasts in the accommodation methods.

Candidates will probably be expected to present their fingerprints (biometric information). Kids under the age of 12 are absolved from finger impression information assortment. Candidates who have presented their fingerprints within the most recent 59 months will undoubtedly not be approached to resubmit.

Candidates might be expected to return on one more date for a meeting in regard to their excursion.

Pay the visa application charge.

flag

When to Apply

Applications should be submitted something like 15 days before the movement date yet not sooner than a half year before the movement date.

Where to Apply for a Poland Schengen Visa

Applications ought to be submitted either through the Clean Office or a visa application focus that is associated with Poland.

Applications ought to be submitted exclusively in the nation of citizenship or home.

In nations with no Clean department, applications might be submitted through a Schengen state department addressing the interests of a Clean office.

Poland Visa Handling Time
It requires around 15 days to handle Poland Schengen visa applications. Nonetheless, at times it could require up to 60 days.

For endorsed visa applications:
Candidates should guarantee that the data on the visa is finished and legitimate upon assortment.

Candidates who have accepted their Schengen Visa for Poland ought to recall the following things:

Illuminate the Clean Department regarding any change to your schedule after accommodation is finished.

The endorsement of a Schengen visa doesn't ensure passage to Poland or different nations in the Schengen region.

Extra reports relating to your monetary means or convenience might in any case be expected to acquire section to Poland or other Schengen regions.

For denied visa applications:

On the off chance that your application for a Poland Schengen visa is dismissed, you reserve the privilege to pursue the choice in 14 days or less.

The allure should be submitted to the emissary that dismissed the visa.

On the off chance that the dismissal is maintained by the representative, a last solicitation can be submitted through a similar emissary to the Commonplace Managerial Court in Warsaw.

There is no expense for the allure demand. Nonetheless, candidates who decide to continue with a last allure through the Clean Courts are expected to pay an expense that can be discounted in unambiguous cases. Notwithstanding, it is non-refundable as a rule, whether your allure is denied or endorsed.

20 Tips for Low-Budget Travel Around Poland

On the off chance that you travel with low spending plan - focus on it!
Tracking down modest accommodation in Poland

Poland is simply brimming with inns, lodgings, and guesthouses. Some of them are completely accessible on Booking.com. Other, particularly those situated beyond enormous urban communities, are generally recorded on nearby sites, for example, Noclegi. pl, which are for the most part accessible just in Clean.

From our experience, PLN 120-150 (25-35 euro) is a standard cost for a twofold room (with breakfast). Nothing extravagant, however, you can definitely track down a less expensive choice, particularly unavailable or beyond huge urban communities. A bed in a residence can be reserved for PLN 25-35 (6-7 euro).

Booking ahead of time?
In the event that you like solace and can't envision spending your days off setting up camp, plan your excursion ahead of time.

Particularly on the off chance that you might want to spend it in a comfortable, delightful guesthouse. The nearer it is to the season, the more modest opportunities for progress.

In high season (July - August) pretty much each and every guesthouse, cabin, or inn anticipates that you should lease a spot for no less than multi week. Booking a spot for Just a weekend is beyond difficult. Additionally, a few spots are reserved far ahead of time, for instance, these very cool tree houses W Drzewach which are presumably currently reserved for every one of the days of 2018.

In any case, on the off chance that you want to invest your energy in Poland in a major city, similar to Cracow or Warsaw, everything is good to go with booking a more limited remain regardless of whether or not prepared.

What is agroturystyka?

You could have gone over the expression "agroturystyka" which can be meant "rustic accommodation". In this case, you are accommodated by the proprietors of the ranch. You can likewise depend on custom-made meals. It used to be one of the least expensive types of accommodation in Poland. Furthermore, there is still a great deal of where you will get a bed for 10 euros.

Anyway, today agroturystyka is getting increasingly present-day. Segregated woodlands and lakesides of Podlasie or Lubelszczyzna became more well-known among the rich working class. Subsequently, a portion of the spots become something between an inn and agroturytyka - situated in no place, yet with bio food and horseriding classes.

low financial plan travel around Poland
Agroturystyka in Lower Silesia

Couchsurfing in Poland

Couchsurfing is a friendliness administration that permits individuals to remain as visitors at somebody's place. It functions admirably in Poland, so you can definitely check it out. Obviously, it is well known for the most part in enormous urban communities.

Couchsurfing isn't the best thing in the world everybody. Can we just look at things objectively for a moment, not every person is prepared to trust an all-out more peculiar enough to share a level. Be that as it may, in the event that you never attempted it yet and might want to begin presently, make sure to keep a couple of straightforward guidelines of the local area:

Try not to deal with it like a free inn.

Compose however much you could in your online at any point profile before you begin to convey demands.

Ask your companions, who are now on CS, to compose a survey for you - it increases your possibilities of tracking down a host.

Customize your solicitations. There isn't anything more regrettable than lethargic composition.

Furthermore, to wrap things up, read others' profiles and audits from different individuals from the local area to stay away from disappointment or risk of running into the wrong individuals.

In the event that not Couchsurfing, then what?

There are many other neighborliness benefits that work surprisingly better than Couchsurfing. They are typically devoted to explicit gatherings. You are arranging a bicycle trip around Poland? Go after model Warmshowers

Setting up camp in Poland gives you adaptability
Be that as it may, in the event that very much like us you wouldn't fret dozing in a tent, you are one fortunate treat. Poland is ideal for setting up camp, even in nature.

The feature of setting up camp is that you don't need to plan or book it ahead of time. There is in every case some room left at the campground, regardless of whether you spontaneously settle on an end-of-the-week break from the city.

Setting up camp in the wild in Poland
Poland is the perfect balance for devotees of setting up camp in nature. Of course, the standards are not quite as adaptable concerning the model in Scandinavia. Nonetheless, it is generally not forbidden to camp beyond the assigned region.

It is anyway forbidden to camp in public and scene parks. Setting up camp in the forest is likewise not permitted. On the off chance that you might want to make it happen, you ought to illuminate a neighborhood ranger service authority.

Yet, dread not. There are a lot of spots around the country that are not covered with backwoods and are only ideal for your tent.

More than an amazing model is this free campground at Siemianowka Lake in Eastern Poland.

Scrumptious low-spending plan feasting in Poland
Foodies with low financial plans will cherish Poland. Topping off is insanely modest and since Clean individuals love to eat, there is zero chance that you return home hungry.

Simply make sure to practice good eating habits. We guarantee you it is truly simple to purchase new and quality feasts in any event, for under 10 euro.

Stay away from the traveler's menu
A tourist menu is a simple method for selling whatever turns out poorly with local people's stomachs. Just drop it and don't go straight into the snare. They may be modest, yet we emphatically accept that quality ought to be similarly pretty much as significant as the cost. What's more, we definitely don't believe that you should return home and grievance on Clean food!

Leave the touristic region behind. Just around a corner, you will track down fewer groups, better food, and perhaps less expensive costs. Find out where local people feast, for instance, understudies.

Find out where the understudies eat
Understudies are the experts of endurance. Find out where the nearest grounds bistro is. They are generally modest. An extraordinary model Stołówka Nawojka in Cracow.

The splendid side of Poland is that you will find grounds in downtown areas. So investigate, ask on the web or on the road where you can get the best supper.

One more illustration of an understudy dinery is Gospoda Koko, which is found nearly at the Fundamental Market in Cracow.

Bary mleczne in Poland
Bary mleczne (milk bar) is likely the least expensive choice for a ravenous migrant. Because of preferential terms (modest lease and so on), they can serve food in some cases

multiple times less expensive than a legitimate café.

Because of low costs and the great nature of food, bary molecules are frequently really swarmed. You will find there enterprise men on lunch, understudies, beneficiaries, and a wide range of individuals who pine for natively constructed food.

Furthermore, you can definitely relax. It is known as a milk bar, however, these days they serve all sorts of food, such as pierogi, meat hacks, hotcakes, Clean soups, and so forth. The cost begins from 1 euro for a soup and finishes around 3 euro for an entire feast. Bon appetit!

I can suggest milk bars like Mokotowski Bar Mleczny in Warsaw or the totally wonderful Bar Mleczny Kociewiak in Tczew

Society's Motels

You will track down there out and about and in probably the greatest urban areas. They serve generally conventional Clean food. Furthermore, they serve it genuinely. The bits are normally huge.

The ideal illustration of the hotel is Szwejk in Warsaw, Kampania Piwna in Cracow, Karczma Bida.

Likewise, at whatever point you are out and about and in uncertain where to eat, search for a motel with bunches of TIRs stopped around. Transporters realize their course like no other individual and are faithful to the best dineries on their way.

Modest going around Poland

Regardless in the event that you are going to a gathering or solo, consistently figure out the awesome, most productive method of transport.

Greatest urban communities and towns are generally effectively accessible via train or modest transport. You can book a train ticket 30 days ahead of time at the earliest. Also, some of the time the least expensive transport tickets cost under 10 PLN (for instance Polski Transport, Lux Express and that's just the beginning).

Transport tickets are normally sold in tranches. Follow the transport organization's fan page to get to know when the new pool of tickets will show up. This is the second when they are the least expensive.

Likewise, it is worth it to realize that going via train in Poland is truly reasonable. The least expensive charges are presented by local trains thus called TLK. Assuming you are fortunate you could likewise purchase pretty modest boarding passes presented by RyanAir and Part.

Carpooling in Poland
Carpooling is broadly famous in Poland. The clean stage that allows you to track down travelers or drivers to share the expenses of movement is called BlaBlaCar.

It is likewise really considered normal to find a ride by Facebook gatherings. Particularly since BlaBlaCar now and again energizes cash for getting paperwork done for the ride. Be that as it may, to find the right gathering you will most likely need a tip from a nearby.

Bumming a ride in Poland
A much less expensive method for driving between Clean urban areas is obviously past, bumming a ride. It is exceptionally simple to get a ride and we spent a superior piece of

our understudy times bumming a ride between Clean urban communities.

For finding an ideal spot to escape the principal urban communities counsel Hitchwiki.

Trekking sets aside cash
As we would like to think, finding Poland by bicycle is the most ideal choice you can settle on if you in the event that you have a lot of time however restricted sources.

The most stunning pieces of Poland (like Suwalszczyzna, Bieszczady, or Podlasie) are generally segregated places with extremely unfortunate public vehicles. Aside from the primary urban communities (or modest communities it is a reality once in a while difficult to arrive without a vehicle.

An ideal option in contrast to a vehicle is joining a train with a bicycle.

The bicycle permits you to go gradually to the point of truly finding every one of the intriguing puts and individuals on your way. You are not limited by any schedule, and can continuously stop or take a diversion. It likewise keeps you fit.

Chapter 3: Best Time to Visit Poland

Poland is a little country, situated in Focal Europe. With a populace of animal categories, Homo, occupying present-day Poland quite a while back, the nation has had a mind-blowing portion of mankind's set of experiences. More than millennia, this region has seen numerous ages dwelling here, across all principal ages like the Stone Age, Bronze Age, Iron Age, etc. Nonetheless, it is the Slavs, who came to the land around the ninth hundred years, who have had the greatest effect in forming the present status of the country. Subsequent to enduring intrusions of different lines, a Clean Lithuanian district, two universal conflicts, and various long periods of battle because of Nazis, present-day Poland sits solidly as a feature of the European Association. With such a lot of history related to the country, you will undoubtedly see various magnificent engineering wonders spread across, various periods and impacts. This, combined with the extraordinary normal excellence that the nation brags of (mountain framework, timberlands, and sea shores), makes Poland a country that you should visit something like once in your life.

Poland has a calm environment, with every one of the four significant seasons in a year. The colder time of year season is the longest, crossing more than 4 months. While the summers are wet and radiant, the spring and harvest time seasons have the most wonderful circumstances for you to investigate the country. In any case, something disconcerting about the Clean weather conditions is that it is very eccentric, particularly with regard to rain. You can unquestionably encounter an hour of shower anywhere even in the springtime, which should be a genuinely dry season. For quite a long time, the unusualness of the weather conditions made the travel industry in Poland a not so well known road, but rather since the nation turned into a piece of the European Association in 2004, there has been a huge push to attract vacationers to the nation and to great profit.

Probably the most well-known vacationer urban communities in the nation are Warsaw, Krakow, Wroclaw, Poznan, Lodz, and Szczecin, with a great deal of destinations and exercises for sightseers to appreciate. Galleries like the Public Gallery of Warsaw, the Public Exhibition Hall in Krakow, the Historical Center of WWII, and others provide you with a striking record of the historical backdrop of the country. Also, the Palace of the Teutonic Request in Malbork, the Noteworthy Focus of Krakow, the Old Town in Warsaw, and the Old City of Zamosc is only a portion of the astounding memorable designs spread across Poland. A significant number of these are UNESCO World Legacy Locales, which simply lets you know how unimaginably lovely they are and the significance they hold to the nation's and world's set of experiences.

Aside from these stunning designs in Poland, you have many normal attractions too. You can't take your eyes off sights like Bialowieza Woodland, Koscielisko Valley, Szczeliniec Wielki, Deviant Rocks, and Pieniny Mountains Public Park. There are a few public paths, spread all through the country, that take you through different woodlands, lakes, and much more. Throughout the cold weather months, you can enjoy exercises like ski visiting, ice skating, snowmobiling, and sled riding, every one of which is downright enchanting.

Because of the development of the travel industry in the new times, there has been an unimaginable expansion in the number of celebrations overall around the year, adding to the allure of the country. With such a huge amount to investigate in the country, the different open doors make certain to speak to each traveler in Poland.

Top Season: July-August

Slow time of year: November-Walk

Poland In Spring (April-June)
Temperature: The temperature during spring in Poland fluctuates between 2 degrees C and 17 degrees C.

Climate: Spring in Poland begins during the colder month of April yet the season takes a turn for the sunnier, making it ideal for voyaging all over the country. The lowest temperature experienced during this time is 2 degrees C and the most extreme temperature arrives at nearly 17 degrees C. Indeed, it can rain practically any day however the normal precipitation is around 45mm.

Huge Occasions: The Ludwig van Beethoven Celebration is a well-known live event that brings different traditional artists from around the world to act in different shows held in Warsaw. Florianski Fair in Warsaw and Juvenalia in Krakow are the best fairs to investigate road exhibitions, food, music, and other neighborhood attractions. Jewish Social Celebration in Krakow and the Worldwide Road Expressions Celebration in Poznan are the greatest celebrations in the period of June. Each celebration referenced is an incredible method for figuring out various neighborhood societies.

Why you ought to visit presently: Springtime is quite possibly the best season in the country to go around due to the charming circumstances. You actually get to see snow in the early piece of the time yet nature before long fires springing up new varieties all over the place, bringing about a few dazzling scenes. It is an incredible opportunity to visit places like Gdansk, Sopot, Gdynia, and Malbrok.

Things to be aware of before the visit: You most certainly need to convey your woolens this month as the evenings are cold. Since it is the shoulder season, you can undoubtedly go around in financial plan costs.

Tip: In a nation like Poland where you can't foresee any climate, you should take your parka or if nothing else an umbrella with you the entire visit if conceivable.

Poland In Summer (July-August)
Temperature: The temperature during summer in Poland ranges between 12 degrees C and 26 degrees C.

Climate: Summer in Poland is the most incredible regarding daylight yet it is additionally the wettest time of all. The weather patterns are not that sweltering with the temperature remaining in the scope of 12 degrees C and 26 degrees C.

Huge Occasions: The Worldwide Road Craftsmanship Celebration in Warsaw is the biggest open-air celebration in the nation, attracting specialists from every one of the urban communities. Open'er Heineken Celebration, a famous live concert, draws in craftsmen like Scorching Bean stew Peppers,

Synthetic Sibling, Florence, and a lot more from around the world. Junction Live performance is another famous celebration that spotlights conventional people's music from the Tatra Mountains. Great Taste Celebration in Poznan is one celebration that pretty much every food darling ought to have on their list of must-dos since it is a worldwide food celebration where you can taste different cooking styles on a single occasion.

Why you ought to visit currently: Even with the unusual weather patterns, the late spring season sees the greatest number of travelers from around the world. Notwithstanding, the significant motivation to visit this season is the extended periods of sunshine that you get, permitting you to visit different spots on a solitary day.

Things to be aware of before the outing: Since it is a top season, you will get a lot of groups, particularly in significant urban communities like Warsaw, Krakow, and Tarnow. In any case, you can visit less investigated urban communities like Torun, Lubin, and Zamosc this season, to stay away from the very bustling regions.

Tips: You should book your tickets and lodgings well ahead of time as you will not get a lodging once you reach, and on the off chance that at all you get one, that will be an expensive undertaking. Continuously convey an umbrella and a raincoat with you as this is the wettest time of all.

Poland In Pre-winter (September-November)
Temperature: The temperature you get to encounter in pre-winter in Poland is

somewhere close to 5 degrees C and 15 degrees C.

Climate: Harvest time in Poland is significantly better compared to summer, regarding how much precipitation. In any case, there is a critical decrease in the temperature particularly in the period of November. The temperature scope of this season is for the most part between 5 degrees C and 15 degrees C.

Huge occasions: Pre-winter in Poland has numerous celebrations for you to appreciate. Warsaw Harvest Time Global Celebration of Contemporary Music, Cross Culture Celebration in Warsaw, and Celebration of Four Societies in Lodz are probably the most well-known celebrations to assist you with experiencing different societies, especially, Clean, German, Russian, and Jewish. Rawa Blues Celebration in Katowice is the world's greatest inside blues celebration. European Celebration of Taste in Lubin is the most incredible as far as giving you a brief look at the food, workmanship, music, and dance culture of Poland.

Why you ought to visit now: Harvest time season is the other shoulder season in Poland, with the long stretches of September to October being awesome to head out around because of more modest groups. Additionally, the costs of the inns and flight tickets are substantially less than the mid-year months. The pleasant foliage during this season, with striking shades of the time popping at you, is an obvious justification for you to visit. Photography sweethearts would adore this season without a doubt.

Things to be aware of before the visit: Despite the fact that it is pre-winter season, there are a lot of celebrations for you to join in. This is likewise an extraordinary time for you to partake in the best Clean cooking as you get well-known treats that are fundamentally important for the mid-year and winter seasons in any case. Kazimierz Dolny, Pieniny, and Kaszuby are a portion of the must-visit places for regular attractions.

Tips: Convey your umbrella consistently because of the eccentric climate Poland tosses at you. Likewise, convey your woolens and perhaps add another layer assuming that you are visiting in November.

Poland In Winter (December-Walk)
Temperature: The temperature stays inside the scope of - 12 degrees C and 4 degrees C in the colder time of year season.

Climate: Winter in Poland can get truly cold and chilling, with temperatures decreasing down to 12 degrees under nothing. The greatest temperature during this four-month time span is only 4 degrees C, which lets you know how cold it can arrive. The nation sees a great deal of precipitation however every last bit of it is chiefly as snowfall. Before genuine winter sets in the urban communities, you can feel the virus winds hitting you over the course of the day. Abrupt downpours can make the day considerably colder.

Huge occasions: Krakow Christmas Dens and Barbican Christmas Market are two of the best Christmas-related festivals in the nation where you get to encounter the Clean culture and customs at their best. Fat Thursday is one celebration that each food sweetheart would love, with an entire day committed to eating and a significant spotlight on desserts like packzi and customary doughnuts.

Why you ought to visit now: On the off chance that you love winter sports, this could end up being one of the most amazing times for you. Zakopane, Izerskie Mountains, and Wisla and Ustron Szczyrk have the best ski resorts in the country. A large number of sightseers run to these objections each colder time of year.

Things to be aware of before the visit: Since the temperature decreases so remarkably, you should wear numerous layers of woolens, including a suppressor, gloves, and thick socks. Likewise, convey a couple of boots to stay away from the frosty temperatures. Aside from Christmas festivities and winter sports, there are very few exercises in the urban communities during this season.

Tips: Since it is unimaginably cool, very few individuals visit Poland this season, bringing about a phenomenal chance for you to investigate the nation and improve on the costs. You can book lodgings and flight tickets at the most reduced potential rates.

Chapter 4: 1 Week in Poland: An itinerary for first-time visitors

Planning your first trip to Poland and don't know where to begin? This 1 week in Poland itinerary takes you on tour to some of the most popular places in the country. Starting the trip in Kraków and finishing it in Warsaw, allows you to expand your trip at either end and see more of Poland. Also, it includes a visit to Auschwitz, Wieliczka, Zakopane, and Torun.

Disclosure: Please note that this post contains affiliate links. This means that if you click on a link marked with [AD] and proceed to make a purchase, I may earn a small commission at no extra cost to you.

Getting Ready for 1 Week in Poland

My 1 week in Poland

This itinerary is based on my 1-week visit to Poland during the summer of 2016 (late August to early September to be exact). Hence, this itinerary mostly applies to visits during the summer. My boyfriend and I flew from Cyprus to Warsaw using LOT Polish airlines and then we took the train to Kraków, as we realized that the most interesting places were closer to Kraków than Warsaw.

We were traveling on a low to midrange budget, but because Poland is relatively cheap we could get some upgrades with the same amount of money we would spend in other cities, such as 4* instead of 3* hotels in the city center and even an organized tour in Auschwitz and Wieliczka Salt Mine, so that we don't have to bother with bus/trains and to be able to visit both in a day.

Day 1 – Kraków

Allow a morning to arrive in Kraków and settle into your accommodation. Then head to the old town to grab something to eat and start exploring the city.

Town Square in Krakow

14:00 Barbican

Visit during the summer months, and you will have the chance to get into the Barbican, one of the many medieval fortifications that used to exist in the city.

Find out more about Barbican here.

14:30 City Defence Walls

Use your Barbican ticket to ascend a part of the nearby remaining city defense walls that were used during the 13th century.

15:00 St. Mary's Basilica

A Gothic-style medieval church in the old town square of Kraków. It dates back to the 14th century and forms part of the UNESCO World Heritage List. Make sure to be there on the hour to hear the distinctive sound of Hejnał Mariacki – the trumpet calls heart in every direction of the basilica.

15:30 Sukiennice (Cloth Hall)

It is referred to as the "world's oldest shopping mall", and it features a large collection of souvenirs in the main Market Square. If you are short on time, return later in the evening as the hall stays open until 9 pm. On the upper level of the hall, there is the Sukiennice Museum, a gallery of 19th-century Polish art.

16:00 Town Hall Tower

Another medieval Gothic-style building in the Old Town of Kraków. The tower is the only remaining of the old town hall and today is part of the Historical Museums in Kraków. Visitors can ascend to the top floor and marvel at the views over the city along with viewing access to the mechanism of the tower clock.

17:00 Collegium Maius

Part of the Jagiellonian University, Collegium Maius is the oldest building of the complex dating back to the 14th century. Today, there is a museum that shows medieval representations of lecture halls, libraries, old scientific instruments, and more. Note that the museum is only open in the afternoons on Tuesdays and Thursdays.

18:00 Wander in Old Town

Finish the day with a horse-drawn carriage ride in the old town and a traditional Polish dinner in one of the many restaurants in the old town.

Directions:

Day 2 – Kraków – Zakopane – Kraków
Spend a day in the Tatra mountains, in Zakopane, the winter place-to-be in Kraków. It has everything from lovely chalets to ski pistes and chimney cakes. In the summer, you can enjoy some lovely walks in nature and admire gorgeous views from the summit. Don't forget to bring a jacket as it can get quite chilly up there.

View of Zakopane
08:30 Kraków Bus Station
The easiest way to reach Zakopane is to take the 2-hour bus to the mountains. Once you get there, you will have to walk a bit to reach

the town center. The map below provides directions.

11:00 Gubałówka Funicular Station
Take the funicular to get to Gubałówka Mountain, 1123 m above ground. There you can find many cute shops and cafes, and you can enjoy amazing views over Zakopane. Walk a little bit around before returning back to Zakopane. You can return using the same funicular as before, or you can walk a little bit further and use one of the two chair lifts: Szymoszkowa or Butorowy Wierch. Szymoszkowa is 15 minutes away from the funicular and can fit up to 6 people per lift, while Butorowy Wierch is 30 minutes away and can only fit 2 people.

Hint: Have a map with you if you're returning from Butorowy Wierch and be prepared to walk! When we visited, we bought tickets for Butorowy Wierch without realizing that there were two chair lifts and this was the one further away. We only found out, when we arrived at Smoszkowa and were told that there was another chair lift further away. However, the struggle was real when we had no idea if we were on the correct route since there was nothing else around, we had no map – roaming without extra charges was not a thing in 2016, and locals didn't speak English very well. Long story short, we found the chair lift, and although it was a bit scary to be hanging from that wire, the views were extraordinary! Oh, the best part was when we had to walk for 50 minutes to get back to Zakopane!

13:30 Walk around Zakopane
Walk a bit in the town center and get something for lunch before continuing your day.

15:00 Kasprowy Wierch Cable Car

Get ready to get to the highest peak in Poland at 1987 m at the border with Slovakia. To get there, you need to take the cable car from Zakopane and change to Myślenickie Turnie (1325 m). The base cable car is an hour's walk from the Zakopane center, but luckily there is a (paid) shuttle bus that takes you there from the Zakopane bus station in just 15 minutes (not very frequent). Once you reach the top, take some time to walk to the highest building in Poland and why not follow a short walking route from there? The views over the Tatra mountains are breathtaking.

Hint: The line to the cable car can get very long in the mornings, so it's better to visit in the afternoon. On our trip there, we decided to change plans and visit it in the morning. It proved to be the wrong decision, as the queue was very long. After waiting for an hour, we decided to abandon the queue (we were about halfway) so that we had time to visit the Gubałówka. However, we returned in the afternoon to check the queue again, and this time there was no queue! We got up very quickly, and at least we managed to spend a few minutes there before going back. (We would like to have more time there, but with all the time we lost waiting in line, leaving the place, and then going back we had barely 20 minutes to the top.)

17:00 Zakopane Bus Station
Early in the evening take the bus to return to Kraków.
Directions (Zakopane and Gubałówka):
Note: The route between the Polskie Koleje Linowe S.A. Stacja Dolna Gubałówka and Funicular – Gubałówka will be covered by the funicular. The same is true for the other way. On the map, both chair lift stations are

shown: Górna Stacja Wyciągowa and Polana Szymoszkowa for Szymoszkowa top and base stations respectively; and Butorowy Wierch Górna Stacja Kolejki Linowej, Mountain Cable Car Butorowy Wierch for the Butorowy Wierch top and base stations respectively. The route to Kasprowy Wierch can also be covered by bus.

Day 3 – Kraków – Auschwitz – Wieliczka – Kraków

Be prepared for an emotional day as the morning involves visiting Auschwitz I and Auschwitz II – Birkenau concentration camps. A guide will take you to the different areas of the Nazi concentration camp and will detail the horrible events that took place there. In the afternoon, the atmosphere is more relaxed with a visit to the Wieliczka salt mines. To visit both places in one day, I recommend taking a tour since public transport connecting Auschwitz and Wieliczka can take at least 2.5 hours.

Block 4 in Auschwitz
10:00 Auschwitz
Auschwitz was used as a concentration camp by the Nazi Germans during World World II. It consisted of many buildings in a large radius. Today there is a memorial and museum at the site, and visitors can walk in the grounds of Auschwitz I and Auschwitz II-Birkenau camps. It is best to visit the place with a guide. Auschwitz-Birkenau is a UNESCO World Heritage Site.

15:00 Wieliczka Salt Mine
Another UNESCO World Legacy Site. It used to be perhaps one of the most seasoned places that delivered table salt, prior to halting its creations in the mid-2000s. Presently, it is one of the most famous vacation spots in Poland, highlighting figures

and sculptures made of salt as well as different displays about the development of salt. To enter the mine, guests need to dive 350 moves to arrive at an underlying profundity of 135m subterranean. The traveler course goes on for around 3km and visits different topical rooms.

Note: On the off chance that you visit the above as a component of a coordinated visit, the hours and request of visiting them might shift. Contingent upon the visit booked a directed visit may likewise be incorporated at each site.

Day 4 - Kraków - Warsaw
This is the last day in Kraków, where there is an ideal opportunity to visit the Wawel Palace and partake in some time at the Vistula Waterway. In the afternoon take the train to go to Warsaw.

10:00 Wawel Palace

Begin your day by visiting this UNESCO World Legacy site, known for its authentic importance. The palace used to house the different lords of Poland, however today it has been changed into a craftsmanship exhibition hall of compositions, armor, earthenware production, and more.

The palace is very huge and needs an opportunity to investigate, as there are five brief shows: the State Rooms, the Regal Confidential Appartements (just available with a visit), the Crown, Depository and Ordnance, the Lost Wawel and Oriental Workmanship. Contingent upon the climate, you can likewise visit the Mythical Serpent Lair and the Sandomierska Pinnacle. Remember to stroll in the open grounds of the palace.

15:00 Meander at the Vistula Stream

For your last action in Kraków, why not stroll along the Vistula Waterway or take a boat visit to Wonder Wawel palace according to an alternate point of view?

17:00 Galeria Krakowska
Subsequent to gathering your baggage structure at your convenience and in the event that have the opportunity before your train withdraws, pass by Galeria Krakowska, a shopping center inverse the train station for any last-minute purchases.

17:30 Kraków Główny
Treat the above time with care as it relies upon your takeoff time. Try to show up sooner than expected at the station as there is just a single train each hour to Warsaw.

20:30 Warszawa Centralna
Show up in Warsaw late at night and sink into your convenience.

Bearings (for Kraków):

Day 5 - Warsaw
Partake in your most memorable day in Warsaw by visiting the "not-really old" town as well as a gallery in the early evening.

Old Town Warsaw
10:00 Palace Square
Begin your day at the Palace Square. At the point when I visited Warsaw, we did one of those free strolling visits around the old town. They were exceptionally enlightening, and we gleaned some significant experience about the region and its kin like Chopin and Marie Courie. The most great reality that we learned was that the Old Town Commercial Center was altogether reconstructed after it was completely annihilated in WWII to look like the first one and consequently, protect its authentic importance. Along these lines, go

for some time and stroll around and see what you can realize.

15:00 Copernicus Science Center

In the early evening, we visited the Copernicus Science Center, the biggest science exhibition hall in Poland. However, in the event that science isn't your thing that is alright, in light of the fact that there are twelve different historical centers that you can visit. One show that we truly needed to visit, yet didn't figure out how to track down (!) was the Undetectable Display which provides you with a thought of the battles that visually impaired individuals face. Different galleries you can visit are the Historical Center of Warsaw, the Public Gallery in Warsaw, the Regal Palace, and the Fryderyk Chopin Exhibition Hall. On the other hand, you can cross the Vistula Stream and visit the memorable and social locale of Praga.

Bearings:

Day 6 - Warsaw - Torun - Warsaw
Go through the day in Torun, a city 2.5 hours from Warsaw. Torun is the origin of Copernicus, a trailblazer protector of the cutting-edge planetary group model.

Torun, Poland
08:00 Warszawa Centralna
Take a morning train to Torun from the focal station. When you show up in Torun Główny, you should stroll about 30 minutes to arrive at the archaic town as the need might arise to cross the Vistula Stream. The guide beneath gives headings. On the other hand, you can take one more train to Torun Miasto, yet you will in any case have to stroll for around 15 minutes.

11:30 Place of Nicolaus Copernicus

The first stop of the day is the place of the well-known space expert Nicolaus Copernicus. The spot recounts the tale of Copernicus, as well as the historical backdrop of Torun during the years that Copernicus lived there.

12:30 Old Municipal Center
A structure of extraordinary verifiable importance houses a little gallery about Gothic Craftsmanship as well as an assortment of pictures. At the highest level, there is a perception deck to respect the city from the top.

13:30 Stroll around the Archaic Town
While going to the following stop, invest some energy strolling in the Middle age Town of Torun (a UNESCO World Legacy Site beginning around 1997) with its charming houses, shops, and cafés and track down a spot to eat.

14:30 Tony Halik Voyagers' Exhibition Hall

A gallery committed to the Clean traveler Tony Halik. It houses displays that Halik brought back from its undertakings all over the planet as well as photos of his movements.

15:30 The Historical Center of Torun Gingerbread

Torun is very notable for its gingerbread, so a historical center about its set of experiences and how it is uttered sounds like a must-visit fascination. Length three stories, the exhibition hall situated in an old gingerbread plant greats guests with the flavor of ginger and a few pieces and pieces about the gingerbread business.

Figure out more about the Gallery of Torun Gingerbread here.

17:00 Torun Główny

Promptly at night, take the train to return to Warsaw with perhaps a pack or two of gingerbread rolls!

Headings (for Torun):

Elective: There are different urban communities too that are near Warsaw and are great for a road trip, like Gdańsk and Łódź.

Day 7 - Warsaw

Partake in your last day in Poland by visiting the tallest structure in the nation and investing some energy shopping in one of the biggest diversion scenes in the city.

Horizon of Warsaw

Horizon of Warsaw. The structure on the left of the picture is the Castle of Culture and Science. Source: Pexels

10:00 Castle of Culture and Science

Perhaps of the tallest structure in Europe at 237m level houses different amusement and instructive scenes. What draws in many guests is its observatory and patio on the 30th floor, which offers uncommon perspectives over the city.

13:00 Złote Tarasy

A shopping center point in Warsaw, just a few minutes from the Royal Residence of Culture and Science. This retail plaza has around 200 shops and eateries, as well as a film and an inn. Likewise, close to the focal train station, its area is great on the off chance that you are utilizing the station to go to the air terminal or to proceed with your excursion to a close by city!

Headings:

Szczesliwej Podrózy!

P.S. This is a new (improved) configuration to introduce schedules, where I incorporate a few data about the attractions and furthermore a Google Guide with bearings for every day. I'm continually checking on the arrangement of my articles, so assuming that you have any ideas on the best way to further develop them, let me know!

Chapter 5: 20+ Best Things To Do In Poland

In the core of Focal Europe lies the second biggest Slavic country Poland. The nation is one of the less popular areas getting well known with voyagers searching for a strange encounter. Poland is the ideal spot for an excursion with your loved ones, for it brings a ton to the table. The nation is home to amazing miracles going from snow-clad mountains to quiet sea shores. These are additionally combined with rich history and scrumptious luxuries tracked down no place in Focal Europe. We have ordered a rundown of the top 20+ best activities in Poland while An extended get-away that you can follow.

20+ Best Activities In Poland

Navigate The Auschwitz Historical Center

The Auschwitz Exhibition Hall is a sign of the Auschwitz Death camp, set up by Nazi Germans during The Second Great War in Poland. The exhibition hall discusses the detestations individuals of Poland needed to endure on account of the Germans and furthermore one of the well-known Poland attractions. The gallery is a huge diary of the set of experiences and the battles that the Clean public went through for their country. There is a motivation behind why it is positioned in the rundown of best activities in Poland.

Area: Więźniów Oświęcimia 20, 32-603 Oświęcim, Poland

Best time: May and October

Passage Expense: Section is Free (charges for guide)

Star Tip: Book an English-directed visit for the best insight

Track The Beskids

The Beskids or the Beskids mountain is an exceptionally famous spot to visit in Poland well known among climbing and traveling fans. The mountain lies in the Carpathian mountain range in the south of the nation, home to a few marvels. The Beskids offers its guests a special jump into the regular excellence that the normal scene of Poland brings to the table. The mountain ranges are home to numerous authentic models protected over the ages with the area positioned high up in Best activities in Poland.

Area: Carpathians mountain range, Poland

Best time: May and October

Section Expense: Open for all

Genius Tip: Book a directed traveling visit for the best perspectives

Step Out In The Gdansk Old Town

The following up of 20+ best activities in Poland carries us to Gdansk Old Town. The town is truly outstanding and the most entrancing Poland traveler places in the country. Gdansk Old Town is home to structures that exude lovely German and Scandinavian-style engineering. These compositional wonders are reminders of the town's long and rich notable mix of different social and ethnic hybrids.

Area: In the northern piece of the Śródmieście region

Best time: May and October

Section Charge: Free (a visit across the town will set you back)

Master Tip: Book an English-directed visit for the best insight

Walk The Tatra Mountains
One of the conspicuous areas for traveling and seeing the all-encompassing perspectives on Poland is the Tatra mountains. The trip to the dazzling pieces of the mountains is about 230 km extended length, which is a long stretch and one of the best activities in Poland. In any case, the perspectives from the highest point of the mountains are one that ought not to be missed. Tatra mountains on both the Clean and Slovak sides are home to a few ski resorts that are impeccably intended for the long cold weather months.

Area: Eastern Carpathian mountain range

Best time: May and October

Passage Charge: Free (pay for a visit)

Genius Tip: Book an English-directed visit for the best insight into the area

Pass-Through The Masurian Lake Locale
Focal Europe's most famous and notable lake locale lies in Poland at the Masurian Lake Area. The lake is a problem area among local people and travelers searching for a bold time frame and a well-known Poland fascination. The lake draws in water sports devotees from various nations all over the planet for a few exercises like drifting, paddling, calculating, and more. The encompassing region of the lake is proper for bikers and nature darlings.

Area: Clean Pojezierze Mazurskie, lake region

Best time: May and October

Section Charge: $ 5 (extra for directed visits)

Master Tip: Book an English-directed visit for the best insight into the district

Take A Visit to The Malbork Palace
One of the 20+ best activities in Poland is to take a visit through Malbork Palace. The palace is one of the biggest on the planet and is quite possibly the most conspicuous and well-known structure in all of Poland. The palace is a fundamental representative design that holds an exceptional spot in Clean culture and a the most ideal getaway destination in Poland. The explanation for the significance is that Clean local people invest wholeheartedly in the design which remains steadfast as an image of versatility. It was at this palace in 1410, that the Clean and

Lithuanian armed forces had the greatest fight in archaic history and the Clean armed forces arose successfully.

Area: Starościńska 1, 82-200 Malbork, Poland

Best time: May and October

Section Charge: $ 10 (incorporates sound aide) (Monday passage is free)

Expert Tip: Which month you pick, go at night to get the light and sound show

Witness the Powerful Buffalo In The Bialowieza Backwoods

The Bialowieza woodland is home to quite possibly the biggest warm-blooded animal that considers Europe its home, the European Buffalo. The buffalo are frequently alluded to by local people as the rulers of Puszcza

Bialowieska. The woodlands are home to around 8,000 500 of these monster furry bovines. As in the mid-twentieth 100 years, they were almost driven to the edge of termination because of exorbitant hunting. However, on account of neighborhood protection endeavors, their number is by all accounts quickly returning.

Area: Podlaskie Voivodeship, Poland

Best time: May and October

Section Expense: $ 20

Ace Tip: Visit the woodland's safe region for a surefire perspective on the European Buffalo

Stagger On The Islands in Wroclaw
Famous activities in Poland take us to the islands of Wroclaw's old town that untruth

spread across the various islets on the Oder Waterway. The great and wonderful islets are connected with one another by a progression of curved spans, that add to the locale's magnificence. The lovely extensions, the cobblestone roads, and the gothic-style houses of worship achieve the best middle-age arrangement there is in a Poland vacationer place.

Area: Wyspa Piasek, Wrocław, Poland

Best time: May and October

Section Charge: N/A

Expert Tip: Book an English-directed visit for the best insight into the district

Snowboard In Zakopane
One of the 20+ best activities in Poland is to visit the well-known vacation destinations of

Poland. One such area is the notable winter resort or a mid-year escape in the core of the Tatra mountains, Zakopane. The area is home to a few regular marvels like cascades, high backwoods, snow-covered tops, uneven lakes, interesting towns, and a lot more normal miracles. Making the objective an extraordinary one for voyagers arranging their excursion to the nation of Poland.

Area: Southern Poland

Best time: May and October

Section Expense: $ 2

Expert Tip: Take and plunge at the Bania warm showers for a reviving encounter

Come By A Milk Bar
Milk Bar

One of the most interesting pieces of a journey to an unfamiliar land is the valuable chance to enjoy previously unheard-of dishes and drinks. Poland as a vacation destination takes this pattern somewhat further and makes it very reasonable. Across Poland, one would find little foundations called 'Milk Bars'. The purpose of setting up these little diners was to permit nearby Clean laborers speedy admittance to reasonable dinners with their restricted wages. Throughout the long term these 'Milk Bars' have become watchmen of the Clean food, which is pretty much genuine in these home-style restaurants.

Area: Numerous areas across Poland

Best time: May and October

Passage Charge: Free (you just compensation for the food you request)

Expert Tip: Make a point to attempt their nearby hand-crafted soups

Loosen up On The Hel Landmass

In spite of its name Hel Landmass positions on top of the best activities in Poland. The area is quite possibly the most hypnotizing place in Poland which is a sanctuary for ocean-side darlings. The area is home to a significant length of brilliant sandy sea shores with lavish green ridges in the setting and a notable Poland vacation place. The Baltic Ocean further upgrades the tranquil marvels of the promontory, with a little fishing town in charge of the landmass extending out into the ocean.

Area: Pomerania territory

Best time: May and October

Section Charge: N/A

Master Tip: Scuba plunge around the waterfront marvel and witness the rich marine life

Meander Around Krakow Old Town

The following action on the rundown of 20+ best activities in Poland is to wander around Krakow Old Town. The city is one of the better-known objections in south Poland and is known for its rich history both famous and threatening. Krakow is one of those urban communities in Poland that takes you on an experience through its roads and prevails upon you with its gothic-style engineering. While garnishing the outlines of spots to visit in Poland.

Area: Southern Poland

Best time: May and October

Section Charge: N/A

Expert Tip: Try not to go during the top season for the best insight

Scout The Slowinski Public Park
The following movement on the rundown of 20+ best activities in Poland carries us to Slowinski Public Park. The area is a significant traveler objection in Poland and is known for its renowned ways of the world. Slowinski Public Park lies along the Baltic shoreline of Northern Poland and lies in the Pomerania area. The recreation area is famous for a few of its ocean-side miracles like peat swamps, glades, woods, and a lake framework. Be that as it may, the main component of the recreation area is the moving ridges tracked down not just in Poland, but in all of Europe.

Area: Pomerania territory

Best time: May and October

Section Charge: $ 2

Master Tip: Recruit a bike for the day to arrive at the recreation area

Float away In The Roads Of Warsaw Old Town
On the rundown of the 20+ activities in Poland, a visit through the roads of Warsaw is sure to be on the cards. The city is home to cobblestone roads made after The Second Great War, trying to reestablish the city to its previous magnificence after the annihilation caused during the conflict. The city's cobblestone roads and gothic designs act as an entryway back into the Middle age ages.

Area: Warsaw, Mazovia Territory, Poland

Best time: May and October

Passage Charge: N/A

Ace Tip: Book an English-directed visit for the best insight

Witness Old Poland In Zalipie
An outing to the little town of Zalipie is perhaps of the best thing to do in Poland. The town is an exceptionally well-known area among voyagers hoping to investigate the brilliant side of Poland. The town is home to little houses that have walls and ovens finished with tiles portraying botanical engravings of various varieties and sizes. The houses additionally depict plans going from crepe paper blossoms, paper cut plans, and roughage insects.

Area: Dąbrowa Region, Lesser Poland Voivodeship

Best time: May and October

Passage Charge: Different visit bundles

Expert Tip: Remember to click a few pictures, with you close to them

Invest Some Energy At The Sanctuary Of Skulls

One of the 20+ best activities in Poland is visiting the 'House of Prayer of Skulls' or 'Kaplica Czaszek'. The congregation lies a kilometer toward the north of Kudowa Zdroj and is quite possibly the most captivating objective in Poland. The congregation is home to the skeletal remaining parts of more than 3,000 individuals. Which were gathered by a Czech cleric, Vaclav Tomasek, and J. Langer, the neighborhood undertaker. The assortment incorporates more than 20,000 bones, of which a couple embellish the walls of the congregation. While most of them stay concealed in a tomb in the cellar of the congregation.

Area: Czermna locale of Kudowa

Best time: May and October

Passage Charge: $ 180 (for a directed visit)

Ace Tip: There is no photography rule inside the sanctuary

Meander Around the Slanted Woodland
The following action on the rundown of 20+ best activities in Poland is to visit Poland's warped backwoods. The region is a woods of north of 400 of these pine forest trees, that take an interesting bend at the storage compartment locale simply over the ground.

The explanation for this interesting occurrence has been a few unique legends and convictions. Yet, until now, no great reason has been made about this extraordinary event.

Area: West Pomerania, Poland

Best time: May and October

Section Expense: N/A

Master Tip: Take a selfie while you are situated in the normal tree seat

Visit The Topsy Turvy House

One of the remarkable activities in Poland when on a get-away to the nation, is to visit the Topsy turvy house. The construction was planned by Clean Humanitarian Daniel Czapiewski, with the house initially made as a piece of workmanship. The Topsy Turvy house was a reference to the socialist time in Poland. Throughout the long term, the work of art has turned into a famous vacation destination, drawing sightseers and local people the same.

Area: Szymbark

Best time: May and October

Passage Charge: $ 12

Genius Tip: Remember to snap a photo of the house from the patio

Investigate The Warsaw Gasworks Historical Center

The following best thing to do in Poland is more to do with voyagers with a mixed bag, ready to investigate the bizarre and the unexplored world. The Warsaw Gasworks Gallery is a brilliant spot to investigate the historical backdrop of the Warsaw Gas Organization. The manufacturing plant was built back in 1888 and later turned into a historical center in 1977. The historical center was known for the creation and metering of endless gas lights from the nineteenth to the twentieth hundred years.

Area: Warsaw, Poland

Best time: May and October

Passage Expense: Free

Genius Tip: Not an entrancing spot for youngsters

Take A Traveler To St. Mary's Basilica
St. Mary's Basilica
On the rundown of 20+ best activities in Poland, the following action in line is a visit

to St. Mary's Basilica. The congregation is perhaps of the most powerful and basic construction that stands as a characteristic of Clean history and engineering. Consistently, trumpets are played from the pinnacles of the design and reach a sudden conclusion in the piece being performed. This is a demonstration, and it is a notorious portrayal of the conflict which saw the trumpeter taking a bolt to the neck, suddenly halting the piece that he was performing.

Area: Kraków, Poland

Best time: May and October

Section Charge: $ 2.35

Master Tip: Visit the congregation close to the fruition of great importance for a dreamlike encounter.

Go To See The Warsaw Uprising Landmark Warsaw Uprising Landmark, Best Activities in Poland

To close our rundown of 20+ activities in Poland, we carry you to the Warsaw Uprising Landmark. The landmark is a sign of the outrages and remorselessness that were looked at by the Clean Nation in 1944 because Hilter drove German powers. The Warsaw Uprising Landmark is a design vital for the Shafts who lost their lives in the uprising. You would observe pictures of antiquated Warsaw of how it looked before the conflict and later. A genuine sign of the flexibility and commitment shown by the Clean Nation even with complete destruction.

Area: Warsaw

Best time: May and October

Section Charge: $ 6 (Tuesdays shut)

Master Tip: Catch the short 3D film for a speedy plunge into history.

Chapter 6: 14 Best Places to Visit in Poland

Poland has a history that dates back almost a thousand years, with stunning medieval architecture, remnants of WWII and its devastation, and castles and palaces in every corner of the country.

But this ancient country is also home to expansive national parks, mountains, and lakes, with seemingly endless trails cutting through virgin nature waiting to be explored.

No matter why you're heading to Poland, discover the most stunning destinations with our list of the best places to visit in Poland.

1. Krakow

One of the oldest cities in Poland, Krakow was already inhabited back in the 7th century. Because the city escaped most of the WWII destruction that fell on other Polish cities, Krakow's Old Town Center still retains its stunning medieval architecture. The Wavel Castle and the historic district of Kazimierz – also known as the Old Jewish Quarter – in the area are both designated as UNESCO World Heritage Sites.

Krakow is home to around 40 urban parks, including 19th-century Planty Park, which covers an area of 21 hectares and forms a green ring around the city center, and the Lasek Wolski forest, which offers hiking and biking trails in a large woodland area just minutes from the city center.

On rainy days, Krakow's 28 museums are a must-see, especially the National Art Collection at the Wawel, where visitors can also see period furniture, a massive collection of Flemish tapestries, the royal jewels, and a collection of weapons and armor dating back to the 15th century.

For an unusual, in-depth look into ancient Krakow and its streets, there's the Rynek Underground Museum.

A number of major attractions and things to do are located outside the city and are popular as day trips. Notable points of interest include the world's oldest functioning salt mine Wieliczka, the Auschwitz-Birkenau concentration camps, and the Tatra Mountains and national park.

2. Warsaw

Poland's capital was left in ruins after WWII – almost 85 percent of its buildings had been turned to ash or systematically razed by Nazi forces. As soon as the war ended, the city embarked on a massive effort to reconstruct its historic center using original plans. As a result, the Baroque and Renaissance merchant houses you see today are perfect replicas of the originals.

Although WWII also caused the loss of collections held by museums and palaces, the city is still home to over 60 museums today. In addition to art and history museums, Warsaw also offers some unusual choices, including the world's only Museum of Posters, a museum dedicated to the WWII Warsaw Uprising, a Neon Museum, and a Museum of Caricature.

The National Museum, which chronicles the history of the city, also houses the largest collection of paintings in Poland – including a number of works of art that came from Adolf Hitler's private collection.

Warsaw might not have as many parks as Krakow, but Lazienki Palace and its formal gardens more than makeup for it. This 18th-century palace is surrounded by 76 hectares of urban forest and is home to a planetarium, an outdoor theater, pavilions, and much more.

For a very different outdoor adventure, walk down Krakowskie Przedmiescie, Warsaw's best architectural street. Old homes, monuments, the Presidential Palace, and the Polish Academy of Sciences are all steps from each other here.

3. Tatra Mountains

The Tatra Mountains and National Park form a natural border between Slovakia and Poland, though most of the mountain range falls into Slovakia. Because there are no borders between EU countries anymore, it's now possible to hike between countries easily. The Polish side of the park has over 270 kilometers of hiking trails.

Poland's highest mountain, Rysy, is located in the Polish Tatras. At 2,500 meters, it's the highest Tatras peak in either country that can be climbed without a park guide. In addition, the park is home to over 600 caves, with the limestone cave system, Wielka Sniezna, being the longest (23 kilometers) and deepest (824 meters).

The Tatras have waterfalls, streams, and mountain lakes. Morskie Oko Lake is the largest lake in the park. Located deep within the park, it can only be reached after a two-hour hike through hills and a thick forest of Swiss pines.

4. Wroclaw

The city of Wroclaw hasn't always been Polish – over the centuries, it has belonged to everything from the Kingdom of Bohemia to Prussia to Germany. Wroclaw has only officially been part of Poland since 1945 after the end of WWII changed some of the border lines in Europe.

The Lubomirski Museum is a good place to visit to learn more about the history of the city – the museum covers the invasion of the city by Nazi forces and later the Soviet Union, as well as a number of WWII events. The Wroclaw City Museum completes that history with an overview of Wroclaw over the past 1.000 years.

Wroclaw's oldest area is the 13th-century Main Market Square, which includes St. Elizabeth's Church and the Old Town Hall. Just a few steps away is the Pan Tadeusz Museum, with multimedia exhibits dedicated to Polish customs.

In summer, visitors can hop on open-top historic buses to travel around the city. Those exploring on foot can search for Wroclaw's dwarfs – over 350 tiny bronze figurines of elves can be found throughout the city, hiding around corners, on sidewalks, and on lampposts.

5. Bialowieza Forest Reserve

Europe's largest remaining section of the primeval forest that once covered much of the continent, the Bialowieza Forest Reserve has definitely earned its designation as a UNESCO World Heritage Site. The forest sits on the border between Poland and Belarus – a border crossing for hikers is actually located within the forest itself – and covers an area of over 1,400 square kilometers.

Bialowieza is a bird-watcher's paradise, and aficionados can join bird-watching tours headed by local ornithologists, but the forest is also home to bison and other large species.

The small village of Bialowieza is within the forest, and so is the open-air Museum of Wooden Architecture – windmills, wooden huts, a tiny wood chapel, a barn, and even a banya (sauna).

6. Bieszczady Mountains

The Bieszczady Mountains are a massive range that extends all the way to Ukraine and Slovakia. They are unique because of their polony (a type of mountain meadow) that only occurs in the Carpathian region. Because the valleys and meadows softly slope up and down – rather than being too steep – they are a perfect destination for hiking.

Polonyna Wetlinska, topping at 1,255 meters, is one of the most famous meadow trails – a picturesque, soft climb that shouldn't take more than two hours. At the top, a small guest house – the only one in the entire mountain range – offers snacks and drinks plus a warm bed for those who want to extend their adventure.

A large section of the Bieszczady Mountains is part of the UNESCO East Carpathian Biosphere Reserve, home to brown bears, wolves, and bison and mostly covered by beech forest.

7. Ojcow

The tiny village of Ojcow, just 16 kilometers outside Krakow, is the gateway to Ojcow National Park. Poland's smallest national park at just 21.46 square kilometers, Ojcow is heavily forested and home to towering limestone cliffs, over 400 caves, and two river valleys. More than 500 species of butterflies inhabit the park – in spring and summer, they take over the trails and the flowering valleys and are a sight to behold.

The Trail of the Eagle's Nests, Poland's most famous tourist and hiking trail, connects 25 castles and watchtowers, including the Renaissance castle at Pieskowa Skala and the ruins of a Gothic castle, both of which fall within the park boundaries. There are also two museums in the park, including a branch of the National Art Collection.

8. Gdansk

Sitting right on a bay on the Baltic Sea, the ancient city of Gdansk is home to Poland's main seaport. Most of the old part of the city – known as the Royal Route – dates back to the 17th century and is beautifully preserved. Some of the main structures here include the City Gates, the Prison Tower, and a number of merchant houses.

Gdansk is also home to the world's largest brick church, St. Mary's, as well as the star-shaped Wisloujscie Fortress and the Gdansk Nowy Port Lighthouse.

Although Gdansk wasn't directly affected by the war, its Museum of the Second World War is one of the best historical museums in the country. It features a number of vehicles – including a Polish Sherman tank and a German DKW motorcycle – as well as artifacts, documents, and photos connected to the war and the Holocaust.

9. Zalipie Village

The tiny village of Zalipie is best known for the folksy flower paintings that adorn almost every building in the area. This tradition started over one hundred years ago when local women used a mix of powdered dye and milk to cover dirty surfaces with colorful designs.

Today, almost every cottage, barn, fence, and even Saint Joseph's church is painted this way – and so are many indoor spaces, including walls and furniture.

Of the many decorated buildings, The House of the Women Painters is perhaps the most stunning. The building is the former home of Felicja Curylowa, an early 20th-century painter born in Zalipie – her entire home, inside and out, is covered with flower paintings and has been converted into a folk museum. The museum showcases the history of the tradition and how the flowers are painted – and visitors even have a chance to try their hand at it.

10. Torun

One of the oldest cities in Poland, Torun's history dates back to the 8th century. Because Torun wasn't bombed or destroyed during WWII, the city's medieval Central Marketplace and its many Gothic houses and wood-beam 16th-century buildings are still standing.

One of these houses is the birthplace of astronomer Nicolaus Copernicus, which has been converted into a museum about the scientist's life and work. The other must-see museum in town is Muzeum Piernika, dedicated to a type of gingerbread unique to Poland, where visitors can try hands-on baking.

The entire Old Quarter area has been designated a UNESCO World Heritage Site – it's a great area to explore on foot, getting lost in little streets to discover the architecture and soul of the area.

Torun's 13th-century Teutonic castle is located here – it is partly in ruins, except for the sewage tower and cellars, as well as a nearby watermill.

11. Isle of Usedom

Since 1945, this island on the Baltic Sea has been legally divided between Poland and Germany. Nicknamed "the sun island" because of how many hours of sunshine it receives every year, Usedom is a popular holiday destination for both countries.

Soft white beaches, seaside resorts, and plenty of summer sports and activities are the main attractions, but the island is also home to a private botanical garden (open only during the warm months), the remnants of the Karnin Lift railway bridge (now designated as a Historic Symbol of Engineering in

Germany), and the Dannenfeldt Mausoleum and cemetery.

Lakes, nature reserves, and manicured gardens are also dotted around the island.

12. Bialystok

With hundreds of stunning old buildings, Białystok will please lovers of both history and architecture. Branicki Palace, built by a wealthy Polish—Lithuanian politician who once dreamed of becoming the king of Poland, is one of the most stunning sights in town – but smaller Hasbach's Palace is also worth a visit.

Make sure to walk around Kościuszko Market Square, surrounded by beautifully ornate townhouses, plenty of cozy cafés, and the Podlachian Museum, mostly dedicated to Polish paintings and art.

On a sunny day, take a walk down Lipowa Street, too, which was almost completely destroyed during WWII and has been restored to become a great place to spot boutique shops and historical buildings.

A branch of the Podlachian Museum, the Historical Museum is an interesting stop to see what a wealthy 19th-century bourgeois home would've looked like — complete with original furniture and objects of the time.

The outdoor Podlachian Museum of Folk Culture offers over 40 traditional wooden buildings to explore (including windmills and a lumberjack's hut) and artifacts like rural transport carriages, forestry tools, and children's toys.

13. Karpacz

This mountain spa town gets its share of visitors in winter, who come here to enjoy skiing on popular Mount Śnieżka. Often referred to as the "winter capital of Poland," Karpacz also offers great ski jumping, snowboarding, and winter hiking.

In warmer months, nearby Karkonosze National Park offers lots of trails.

The main building in town is the 13th-century Lutheran Wang Chapel, made entirely of wood without using any nails. There are also a number of museums, including the Museum of Sports and Tourism about the area's history, a Museum of Toys, and the unique World of Trains, featuring a large collection of railway models.

14. Leba

The tiny village of Leba is one of Poland's best destinations for beach life. Though busy and filled with visitors in summer, Leba retains its lazy vibe, with the rolling sand dunes and the soft waves at the center of the attractions here.

For those wanting more things to do than just sit back and enjoy the sun, there's horseback riding and over 140 kilometers of hiking trails in the area.

With 32 kilometers of coastline, Slowinski National Park is home to "moving dunes," which are carried by the winds and move up to 10 meters a year. It's a stunning vision and a favorite stop for visitors. There are also pine forests and peat bogs to explore here, plus great opportunities for bird-watching.

Chapter 7: 10 Best Polish Foods Everyone Should Try

Clean cooking is much of the time a startling feature of many individuals' excursions because of the country's food culture that is just as rich as other European countries. Stuffed and loaded with flavor and calories, a considerable lot of the best Clean food varieties are rich, substantial, and served in tummy-busting segments. Here are the best dishes in Poland that you shouldn't miss.

1. Pierogi

Pierogi are Clean sickle-formed dumplings that can be bubbled, broiled, or heated and accompany different fillings. The most run-of-the-mill fillings incorporate cabbage and mushrooms, potato and cheddar, or essentially meat - normally pork or hamburger.

A sweet assortment of pierogi is entirely expected by the same token. Among these, the most well-known ones are loaded up with curds and raisins or natural products.

2. Bigos

This cabbage-based stew is a flat-out must on the Christmas table of each and every Clean family. It commonly comprises both new and matured cabbage, various types of meat hacked into pieces, different sorts of Clean wieners, onions, dried timberland mushrooms, and plenty of spices and flavors like narrow leaves, cloves, nutmeg, marjoram, and others.

Various types of meat are viewed as fundamental while making bigos - the more kinds, the better.

3. Placki ziemniaczane

Exemplary potato hotcakes, Placki ziemniaczane are made of a mix of eggs, ground potatoes, and onion, then, at that point, seared in oil until firm. They're presented with various fixings that range from flavorful ones like sharp cream or sauce to sweet ones like fruit purée or sugar.

4. Barszcz

Barszcz is a beetroot soup that can be served either hot or cold and is normally presented with uszka - ravioli-type little dumplings loaded up with meat or cabbage and mushrooms. The recipe fluctuates between various families, and various vegetables like tomatoes or carrots might be added, changing the consistency of the soup contingent upon the nearby practice.

Uszka in a real sense signifies "little ears" - the name comes from the state of the dumplings.

5. Gołąbki

One of the most mind-blowing Shine foods you can attempt is a cabbage roll. Gołąbki is minced meat, cleaved onions, and rice enclosed by a cabbage leaf that makes a kind of envelope or pocket, which is then cooked in pureed tomatoes. This good dish is normally had for lunch or early supper. Gołąbki signifies "little pigeons".

6. Pączki

This staple Clean treat contrasts from what we know as doughnuts in that it doesn't have an opening, yet is a leveled circle of batter commonly loaded up with rosehip jam, vanilla pudding or chocolate, and afterward rotisserie. They are likewise normally covered with powdered sugar or icing and sprinkled with freeze-dried orange zing.

The last Thursday before Loaned is called Tłusty czwartek ("Fat Thursday") in Poland, and one should commend this ongoing gala before the significant stretch of fasting by eating a lot of doughnuts.

7. Żurek

Żurek is a soup made of soured rye flour that typically contains bits of bubbled pork frankfurter and a hard-bubbled egg. It is exceptionally regular during the Easter season and can in some cases be served in a consumable bowl made of bread.

8. Flaki

The name of this soup is derived from its fundamental fixing - dainty cleaned pieces of meat garbage. It ordinarily contains a wide assortment of vegetables and sweet-smelling spices, yet the recipe shifts generally across various districts of Poland.

9. Oscypek

Oscypek is a smoked cheddar made of salted sheep milk, delivered in the Tatra Mountains district. It tends to be utilized as a fixing in meat dishes and mixed greens or eaten all alone as a tidbit. It is then ordinarily barbecued and presented with cranberry sauce.

10. Kiełbasa

The widely popular Clean kiełbasa is essentially a hotdog, yet practically every district of Poland has its own assortment. They can be delivered from various types of meat, have different flavoring and shapes, and can be ready in various ways.

The most famous sorts of kiełbasa are kabanosy (meager, dried pork wiener with caraway seeds), Krakowska (thick, smoked hotdog with pepper and garlic from the Cracow locale) and biała (white frankfurter that is sold uncooked and is much of the time utilized in soups).

This article incorporates assessments of the Go Aides publication group. Hotels.com remunerates writers for their compositions showing up on this site; such pay might incorporate travel and different expenses.

Chapter 8:12 Restaurants In Poland That Will Make You Fall In Love With Polish Cuisine

The most outstanding aspect of culinary workmanship is that it gives and brings just happiness. The person who consumes the range of dishes and the person who sets it up, both experience satisfaction. You will go through a comparative encounter when you make a visit to the cafés in Poland.

Poland, like other European nations, is renowned for the rich culture and customs individuals have been protecting since the days of yore. This culture is reflected in the Clean cooking served in numerous eateries of the country.

12 Best Eateries In Poland

No big surprise, the spot has its personal binds with the sort of food it serves, and the guests are served unconditionally here. You could get confounded while picking the ideal locations to feast at while investigating the country. Around then, go through the rundown we have organized to hold you back from stalling out in such situations.

1. Starka Café

This is one of the most outstanding spots to have conventional food arranged in a really Clean style! The idiosyncrasy followed by the servers as well as the entire spot is basically Clean, carrying you nearer to the way of life of this country. The spot is certainly an extraordinary one to gather a few recollections, no question!

Area: Józefa 14, 31-056 Kraków, Poland

Contact: +48 12 430 65 38

Rating: 4.6 out of 5!

2. Unit Aniołami

To have the option to get astonishing and bother-free insight, we prescribe you book a table before your visit. This one can make your life a smidgen more OK with the selection of dishes accessible and the sort of flavors they use. Not just this, they even attempt to make the specialty of culinary to somewhat explore different avenues regarding

Area: Grodzka 35, 33-332 Kraków, Poland

Contact: +48 12 430 21 13

Rating: 4.4 out of 5!

3. N31 Café and Bar

This spot is known for a few truly cool beverages and the assortment thereof. The food is kept as much fiery as you might want to have. The spot is astounding as a result of the sort of feeling and stylistic layout it has.

Area: Nowogrodzka 31, 00-511 Warszawa, Poland
Contact: +48 600 861 961
Rating: 4.7 out of 5!

4. Restauracja Polska Różana

This eatery too really and dedicatedly mirrors the way of life and customs of Poland through its food. The staff is incredibly cheerful and conveys a Clean lead while serving dishes to the guests.

Area: Chocimska 7, 00-791 Warszawa, Poland
Contact: +48 22 848 12 25
Rating: 4.7 out of 5!

5. Specjały Regionalne

Situated in Warszawa, a decent focal spot and try and can be properly called a center. The flavors are intriguing and make you plunge into the customary flavors. The environment is very dynamic in this eatery. Open-air seating is accessible as well, permitting you to savor the hustle in the city as you enjoy a portion of their fortes.

Area: Nowy Świat 44, 00-363 Warszawa, Poland
Contact: +48 662 254 215
Rating: 4.4 out of 5!

6. Czarna Kaczka

The name of this eatery means "the dark duck", which is additionally its particular dish. The cooks at this spot are known to utilize new fixings. The spot is absolutely marvelous with the sort of assortments it offers in food and drink.

Area: Poselska 22, 31-002 Kraków, Poland
Contact: +48 12 426 54 40
Rating: 4.6 out of 5!

7. Dom Polski

Dom Polski is known for its complex insides. The staff here works nonstop, ensuring you leave with extreme fulfillment with their food as well as administration. The café invests heavily in being a minister of Clean food.

The fixings they pick are nature-motivated and taken by alluding to the customary cookbooks.

Area: Francuska 11, 03-906 Warszawa, Poland
Contact: +48 22 616 24 32
Rating: 4.5 out of 5!

8. Szara Gęś w Kuchni

Here, you get to encounter an extraordinary atmosphere and browse a portion of the astonishing assortments in food. The spot is actually a cool one to bring along your companions and you might in fact come here for gatherings and little parties.

This spot is most popular for its fine wine and exemplary help by a staff that is cordial as well as expert.

Area: Rynek Główny 17, 31-008 Kraków, Poland
Contact: +48 12 430 63 11
Rating: 4.6 out of 5!

9. Fab Combination Eatery

As the name recommends, the gourmet specialists here utilize different fascinating mix of flavors with regard to their dishes. You can view it as Clean, and standard, with awesome tones and taste. Anticipate nostalgic piano music at the scenery, exquisite white lilies, and unpretentious candlelight.

With dishes valued sensibly, this spot is one of the must-visit Clean eateries.

Area: Joselewicza 17, 31-031 Kraków, Poland
Contact: +48 12 442 75 05
Rating: 4.5 out of 5!

Proposed Read: 10 Mind-boggling Sea Shores in Poland To Allow Nature to Relieve You Down!

10. Society Gospoda
Attempt their specially designed dry natural product-filled treat and hand-made cranberry. This spot guarantees quality that can be tasted with each chomp. There are no

designed added substances or flavor enhancers in the dishes they serve. All you'll get is quality, pure food made with affection.

Area: Waliców 13, 00-865 Warszawa, Poland
Contact: +48 22 890 16 05
Rating: 4.4 out of 5!

11. Gościnna Chata

Have delectable fluffy roll and meringue cakes, baked goods with new natural items, hand-crafted cheesecake, dried-up organic product-filled treats, and flavorful frozen yogurt at this spot.

They offer the best champagnes, amazing wines, whiskeys and cognacs, and Clean and provincial vodkas.

The menu integrates cold starters, hot appetizers, and green servings of leafy greens, soups, poultry, fish and meat.

Area: Sławkowska 10, 31-014 Kraków, Poland
Contact: +48 12 423 76 76
Rating: 4.6 out of 5!

12. Café Padre

This café was opened with mind-boggling energy to serve standard Clean foods. Starting from the start, this eatery is dedicatedly serving the best regular Clean dishes.

Presently, they have an even high level of serving foods propelled from all sides of the world.

Area: Wiślna 11, 31-007 Kraków, Poland
Contact: +48 12 430 62 99
Rating: 4.6 out of 5!

Chapter 9: 7 non-touristy cities to discover in southern Poland

Poland, is a wonderful nevertheless a piece underestimated country in Focal Europe. In spite of the fact that it was an off in an unexpected direction objective for a really long time, it is changing quickly at this point. Consistently an ever-increasing number of unfamiliar vacationers visit Clean urban areas. In the south of the nation, Kraków and perhaps Worcław are the most well-known city break objections. You can find out about these spots in pretty much every movement guide. Nonetheless, consider the possibility that you might want to see something beyond these famous places of interest. In this blog entry, I present you a rundown of 7 non-touristy urban communities in southern Poland, where you will feel the nearby environment and see what regular day-to-day existence resembles.

1. Gliwice.
Gliwice Market Square, Poland
Do you have a trip to Katowice Air terminal and considering fascinating things to see close by? Visit Gliwice, one of the most established and lovely urban communities in this piece of Poland. Make certain to go to Market Square and go for a stroll around the little Old Town, where you will track down numerous exquisite eateries and bistros. You can likewise visit the Palm House, the well-known Radio broadcast, and walk the roads of Gliwice, where there are numerous memorable dwellings and delightful old places of worship. Assuming that you might want to learn about this city or simply see more photographs, look at my blog entries:

Top 10 activities in Gliwice, Poland, and 22 winter photographs to rouse you to visit Gliwice, Poland. You can get to Gliwice from Katowice Air terminal by transport AP1, the ticket costs PLN 14 (3-4 euros) and the excursion requires about 60 minutes.

2. Prudnik.

The Market Square in Prudnik, one of the most gorgeous non-touristy urban areas to find in southern Poland

In the event that you might want to visit some little lovely town and climb the mountains, Prudnik in southern Poland will be an ideal objective. Simply take a gander at this lovely Market Square with the Ornate Classicist City Lobby working in the center! Great, right? There are additionally other intriguing spots to see, for example, the Wok Pinnacle, city walls, lovely Lead celestial host Michael Church, and city park. Subsequent to visiting Prudnik, you can go to the close by Opawskie

Mountains. Do you see them in the image? They are on the left. To peruse more about this spot, look at my blog entry: An excursion to the Opawskie Mountains, Poland.

3. Paczków.
Paczków, one of the most astounding non-touristy urban areas to visit in Poland
Paczków is a humble community in southern Poland, which is many times called the Clean Carcassonne. This is on the grounds that Paczków fortresses are the best-safeguarded landmark of metropolitan protective engineering in Poland. There are numerous compositional diamonds and landmarks that are many years old! The best things to see in Paczków are its middle-aged Old Town, protective walls, the Gothic Church of John the Evangelist, and the place of the city killer (Dom Customized structure). There is additionally one of only a handful of exceptional grape plantations in this piece of

the country in Paczków, so on the off chance that you might want to attempt Clean wine, you can do it here!

4. Głuchołazy.

Głuchołazy, a mystery spot to visit in southern Poland

Assuming that you are in Prudnik or the Opawskie Mountains, it is likewise worth visiting the close by Głuchołazy. This humble community was once a well-being resort, where patients were treated with hydrotherapy. The best things to see in Głuchołazy are the Market Square and the Old Town with a checkered metropolitan design demonstrated on a Roman military camp. You ought to likewise check out at the Congregation of St. Wawrzyniec, the Upper Entryway Pinnacle, and go for a stroll around Parkowa Góra, where there is a noteworthy post tower.

5. Tarnowskie Góry.

Tarnowskie Góry, perhaps one of the most gorgeous cities in Silesia, southern Poland Tarnowskie Góry, an unlikely treasure of southern Poland. The city is found just 20 km from Katowice Air terminal and 30 km from Gliwice and Katowice. You can see here both the lovely Old Town and the captivating universe of underground halls and passages. Did you have at least some idea that Tarnowskie Góry has the longest underground boat stream in Poland? On the off chance that you are here, make certain to take a boat ride through the underground halls of the Dark Trout Adit or the Notable Silver Mine. Astonishing experience! Remember to visit Market Square and go for a walk along the roads of the Old Town. The historical backdrop of Tarnowskie Góry traces all the way back to the sixteenth 100 years and there is a ton of intriguing engineering to see.

6. Katowice.

Katowice, Poland - a non-touristy city to find in southern Poland

This city is unique in relation to the others I referenced here. In Katowice, you won't find the archaic Market Square encompassed by notable dwellings or the enchanting old town. Nonetheless, the capital of the Upper Silesian Modern Region brings numerous different things to the table. Did you have any idea that the main high rise in Poland was Katowice? Furthermore, in this city, you will track down many captivating pioneer structures and fascinating road workmanship. Remember to see the Spodek sports and amusement corridor while in Katowice. The Global Congress Community, the structure of the Clean Public Radio Ensemble Symphony, the Silesian Exhibition Hall, and the notable mining settlement of Nikiszowiec are additionally seen.

7. Racibórz.

Racibórz, one of the most outstanding non-touristy urban areas found in southern Poland

Once, this city was a truly building jewel, yet after The Second Great War, it was nearly wrecked to the ground. Blocks from wrecked structures were utilized to revamp the capital of Poland, Warsaw. Today, situated around 50 km from Gliwice, Racibórz isn't a similar city as it used to be, however, it is surely worth a visit. Assuming you have a vehicle and some spare energy, it merits taking a ride here, on the grounds that the street from Gliwice is exceptionally beautiful and leads through woodlands that conceal numerous pearls like the Cistercian Nunnery and the notable restricted check rail line in Rudy. Once in Racibórz, make certain to visit the Market Square and walk the roads of the Old Town. The design here is a genuine blend of various styles, however I think the city is still truly beguiling. Remember to visit Racibórz Palace and attempt Raciborskie lager from the neighborhood bottling works.

Chapter 10: Safety and security

Illegal intimidation

There is a high danger of fearmonger assault worldwide influencing UK interests and English nationals, including from gatherings and people who view the UK and English nationals as targets. You ought to stay careful consistently.

UK Counter Psychological Warfare Policing has data and exhortation on remaining safe abroad and what to do in case of a fear-based oppressor assault. Figure out additional about the worldwide danger from psychological warfare.

Psychological Warfare in Poland

Psychological militant assaults in Poland can't be precluded.

Ukraine line

The FCDO exhorts against everything except fundamental travel toward the western locales (oblasts) of Zakarpattia, Ivano-Frankivsk, Ternopil, and Chernivtsi, and keeps on prompting against all movement to the remainder of Ukraine. For the most recent data, check the Ukraine travel exhortation. There have been Russian military strikes in Ukraine inside 20km of the Clean boundary. In 2022, there was a blast in Przewodów close to the Ukrainian boundary killing 2 Clean nationals.

The fundamental line crossing focuses on entering Poland from Ukraine and can be tracked down on the Ukrainian government site. Plan for expected long postponements at line intersections.

Admittance to within 15 meters of the Clean boundary with Ukraine is limited. Follow this constraint consistently beyond assigned line crossing focuses and adhere to the directions of Clean specialists assuming that you are around here.

Assuming you have shown up in Poland from Ukraine and need help, call +48 22 311 0000 or +44 1908 516666 and select the choice 'consular administrations for English nationals'. You can likewise send an inquiry utilizing the web contact structure.

Belarus line

FCDO prompts against all movement to Belarus. There is restricted admittance along parts of Poland's boundary with Belarus. The Kuznica-Bruzgi street line crossing is as of now shut. In February, traffic was suspended at the Bobrowniki line crossing until additional notification. More boundary-designated spots might close or carry out limitations at short notification and other interruptions are conceivable.

Admittance to inside 200 meters of the line with Belarus is as yet restricted. You ought to comply with this constraint consistently and adhere to the guidelines of Clean specialists in the event that you are around here.

Political circumstances and showings
Public showings are normal. Walks and social events are generally tranquil and very much policed, however, take additional consideration in jam-packed places. Showings can draw in brutality. Screen nearby media and adhere to the guidelines of neighborhood specialists.

Wrongdoing
Racially spurred assaults

Most guests experience no challenges. Serious wrongdoing against outsiders is uncommon, however, violations truly do happen and at times go after have been racially persuaded.

Safeguarding your possessions
Be aware of road wrongdoing and trivial robbery. Outsiders should be visible as obvious objectives. Keep assets and money concealed, particularly:
in jam-packed regions
in places of interest
at fundamental rail stations and on all train administrations and short-term sleeper trains

Informal cab drivers
Informal cab drivers frequently cheat. Travelers have been gone after, including rapes, in informal taxicabs and vehicles booked utilizing ride-share applications. See

further exhortation from the Clean police (in Clean).

Try not to utilize informal cabs. Official cabs will:

have the name and phone number of the taxi organization on the entryway and top of the taxi
show a rate card on the window of the vehicle
Taxis with a peak however no organization name are not official.

Avoid potential risk, especially around evening time or on the other hand in the event that you are separated from everyone else.

Drink and food spiking
Survivors of spiked drinks have been looted in bars and clubs. Be cautious about taking

beverages from outsiders or leaving your beverage or food unattended.

Cheating in bars
Check your bill cautiously while purchasing drinks in bars and clubs. Guests have been cheated enormous sums while paying for drinks by charge or Mastercard.

Rape
There is guidance for casualties of assault or rape in Poland.

Regulations and Social Contrasts
Double nationals
Double Clean English nationals will be treated as a Clean public whenever captured or confined by the Clean specialists.

Liquor regulations

It is against the law against the law to savor liquor in public spots. Whenever got, you may be fined.

In the event that you are savored in a public spot, you could be taken to a facility to be restoratively surveyed. You should remain there until you are clearheaded, including for the time being. You should pay for the expenses of your visit.

LGBT+ explorers

Unassuming communities and rustic regions can be less lenient towards LGBT+ voyagers. There are gay and LGBT+-accommodating cafés, clubs, and bars in numerous towns and urban communities including Warsaw, Krakow, Wroclaw, Poznan, Gdansk, and Sopot.

Same-sex connections are legitimate and same-sex accomplices can live respectively, however, same-sex relationships and common associations are not perceived under Clean regulation.

Jaywalking
You could be fined assuming you are found jaywalking.

Photography
Try not to take photos of military or other security establishments and different structures or things of public framework where there are signs forbidding photography.

Transport chances
Wear intelligent apparel
Walkers and cyclists should wear an intelligent thing around evening time in nondeveloped regions. You might be considered capable in the event that you are engaged in a mishap and not wearing an

intelligent thing. You could be fined 100 Clean zloty (around £20) in the event that you don't have an intelligent thing.

Public vehicle

Approve a public vehicle ticket toward the beginning of an excursion. You will be fined assuming that you travel on an invalid or unvalidated ticket.

Street travel

On the off chance that you want to drive in Poland, see data on driving abroad and read the RAC guide.

Poland is a significant east-west travel course for weighty vehicles. The street network is overall continually redesigned, and roadworks are continuous, especially in summer. Indeed, even a few primary streets between significant towns and urban communities can be limited and ineffectively surfaced, making driving into the evening, especially testing.

Vehicle recruit
Most vehicle rental organizations won't permit you to take your recruited vehicle across the Poland/Ukraine line.

Licenses and allows
You can drive in Poland with your UK photocard driving permit without the requirement for a worldwide driving grant (IDP).

Assuming you're living in Poland, check the Living in Poland guide for data on the standards for occupants.

While driving, consistently have your:
driving permit
ID
vehicle enrollment papers

vehicle possession papers

protection papers

You should show these reports assuming that you are come by the police or on the other hand assuming you cross non-Schengen borders. This incorporates rental vehicles. In the event that you don't have these papers, the police might take your vehicle and charge you for this. On the off chance that you drive a vehicle in Poland, it should meet neighborhood-specialized prerequisites.

Driving an English vehicle abroad

You might require a UK sticker to drive your vehicle outside the UK. From 2021 UK stickers have supplanted GB stickers. Really take a look at the directions on showing number plates for more data on what to do in the event that you are driving external the UK.

Tolls

You might have to pay a street cost for certain pieces of motorways, turnpikes, and public streets. More data is accessible on the cost administrator site.

Top travel and tourism Websites for 2024

Top Travel and The Travel Industry Sites in Poland Positioning Examination for 2024

booking.com positioned number 1 and is the most visited Travel and travel industry site in Poland in January 2024, trailed by rozklad-pkp.pl as the next in line, and wakacje.pl positioning at the third spot as the heads of the Movement and The travel industry sites in Poland.

Deterring the main 5 Travel and The travel industry sites positioning rundown in Poland are koleo.pl positioned in the fourth spot, and intercity.pl at the last situation for January 2024.

Come back again one month from now for the refreshed site positioning and traffic examination of the most visited Travel and travel industry sites in Poland!

FAQs About The Top Travel and The Travel Industry Sites in Poland
Question: Which is the top Travel and travel industry site in Poland?
Reply: booking.com is the most well-known Travel and travel industry site in Poland in January 2024.

Question: Which is the second most visited Travel and travel industry site in Poland?
Reply: rozklad-pkp.pl is the second most visited Travel and travel industry site in Poland in January 2024.

Question: What are the top 5 most famous Travel and travel industry sites in Poland?

Reply: The best 5 most famous Travel and The travel industry sites in Poland in January 2024 are:

1. booking.com
2. rozklad-pkp.pl
3. wakacje.pl
4. koleo.pl
5. intercity.pl.

Conclusion

As we arrive at the last pages of "Poland: Embrace the Concealed," we truly trust this guide has filled in as a wellspring of motivation, disclosure, and joy on your excursion through Poland. Your investigation of this charming nation has been an honor, and we believe that the different schedules, stowed-away undertakings, and social bits of knowledge have upgraded your experience.

Poland's magnificence is diverse, and we trust you've found aspects that resonate with your inclinations and interests. Whether you've meandered through the noteworthy roads of Warsaw, wondered about the middle-age appeal of Krakow, or embraced the oceanic charm of Gdansk, every second is a string woven into the rich embroidery of Poland.

Past the milestones and undertakings, this guide is expected to catch the pith of Clean culture, welcoming you to enjoy customary cooking, take part in neighborhood customs, and associate with the glow of individuals. We accept that genuine travel is a submersion in the spirit of a spot, and we trust these encounters have had an enduring effect.

As you close the book, we urge you to convey the soul of investigation forward. Poland's accounts are consistently developing, and we trust this guide has started an oddity to proceed with your excursion past these pages. Share your encounters, make your own stories, and embrace the inconspicuous corners of this momentous country.

We esteem your input and would respect it if you would pause for a minute to leave a survey. Your considerations and experiences are significant, for us as well as for individual voyagers trying to leave on their own Clean experience. Your surveys assist with molding the eventual fate of this aide and add to a local area of voyagers enthusiastic about investigating the world.

Many thanks to you for picking "Poland: Embrace the Inconspicuous" as your sidekick on this paramount excursion. May your movements forever be loaded up with disclosure, wonder, and the delight of embracing the concealed. Safe ventures, and until we meet again for another experience!

Printed in Great Britain
by Amazon